A Father's Stories For His Children

A Christian Reader
For Students Grades 5-9

Robert Darrol Shanks Jr., PhD

A Father's Stories For His Children
A Christian Reader For Students Grades 5-9
Copyright © 2019 by Robert Darrol Shanks Jr., PhD

All rights reserved. No part of this publication may be reproduced, distributed, or transmitted in any form or by any means, including photocopying, recording, or other electronic or mechanical methods, without the prior written permission of the publisher or author, except in the case of brief quotations embodied in critical reviews and certain other noncommercial uses permitted by copyright law.

Although every precaution has been taken to verify the accuracy of the information contained herein, the author and publisher assume no responsibility for any errors or omissions. No liability is assumed for damages that may result from the use of information contained within.

Unless otherwise indicated, Bible quotations are taken from New International Version (NIV) © 1995 by Zondervan Publishing House and New King James Version (NKJV) MacArthur Study Bible © 1997 by Thomas Nelson, Inc.

Library of Congress Control Number: 2019934285
ISBN-13:   Paperback: 978-1-64398-068-3
           PDF: 978-1-64398-126-0
           ePub: 978-1-64398-127-7
           Kindle: 978-1-64398-128-4
           Hardcover   978-1-64398-129-1

Printed in the United States of America

PUBLISHING

LitFire LLC
1-800-511-9787
www.litfirepublishing.com
order@litfirepublishing.com

This book is in remembrance of our deceased children:

Robert Scott Shanks

Kandace Leigh Shanks

Steven Alan LaSalle

And

Diana Lynn Hontz

Cover photo is of the author's son Robert Scott
and daughter Krystal Lynne

Contents

Grandma McCurdy's Wisdom 1

Listening to That "Little Voice" 5

Of Land Mines and Cardboard Houses 8

Grandma and the Bible 11

Unintended Consequences 14

He Kicked the Bus Tires 17

Those on the Margins of Society 20

We Are Witnesses for Christ in All that We Do 23

What Does Being Humble Mean? 26

How Important Is Attitude in Life? 30

A Father's Gift of Christianity to His Family 34

The Queen and the Other One 37

Intelligence vs. Wisdom 40

God Is a Healing God 44

The Green Porch Swing 48

Accepting Christ as Your Savior 52

A Father and Son Revelation 58

A Ham Sandwich and Coffee! 62

"Quiet, Be Still" 65

Don't Be Ashamed 69

Forty Crosses 72

Our World's Forgotten People -
The Unreached for Jesus Christ! 75

An Ancient Roman Disciple of Christ 78

Grandma McCurdy's Wisdom

Bobby Darrol pumped his bicycle furiously against the stiff Nebraska wind as he made his way across town to see "Grandma Curdy," the most favorite grandma for all the grandkids in his family. It was Saturday, the day he often sat on the porch swing with his grandma to talk about life and all the fun and troubles of being twelve years old.

He knew today was going to be a special day because as he neared her corner he could already smell the fresh baked bread coming from her house and filling the air in the neighborhood. Bobby laid his bike against the white picket fence as he ran up the porch steps and knocked on the door. The door opened to the smiling face of his white haired grandmother, "Hi Grams." She grabbed him and gave him one of her special hugs and said, "Let's have some fresh bread and butter and sit on the porch swing Bobby." In no time the two of them were slowly swinging back and forth on her green wooden porch swing hung from chains enjoying the warm morning sun flooding through the porch screens and eating the warm bread fresh out of the oven. "Grandma, why do some kids tell lies at school to hurt others?" Grandma Curdy's eyes sparkled as she looked at Bobby with that special look of wisdom as she said, "Well Bobby you and I know that we shouldn't lie but the reasons why others do is not for us to worry about. We just need to treat others as we want to be treated and to help others, not hurt them."

She got up and disappeared into the house returning with more warm bread and her little black book tucked under one arm. Bobby was always amazed that no matter how much he didn't understand about a problem, grandma Curdy could always find an answer in that little black book. He really liked these Saturday mornings that he could spend with his grandma and besides she knew everything that he liked to eat too! She made him feel important and he could feel her love and caring. She always made things seem better and not as serious as he thought they were. His mom and dad were important too but there was something special about grandma "Curdy". She slowly thumbed through her book peering over the edge of her glasses to look at Bobby. Finally she found what she was looking for and began to speak. "It says right here that we are to love our neighbor."

"Even though they hurt us?" Bobby said.

"Yes, you see, Bobby, kindness is better than meanness. What should we do when someone tries to hurt us, Bobby?"

"Try to be kind to them even if we don't want to?"

Grandma Curdy said, "Yes, you know what happens if we trade one act of meanness for another, the situation just gets worse doesn't it?"

Bobby shook is head yes as he thought about it.

Grandma's wisdom was amazing to Bobby. He often wondered how she knew so much and was so wise. It was a long time before he knew what that little black book was and what it was all about. When he was eight years old he asked Grandma the name of the book and why she read it and she told him with that characteristic sparkle in her eyes."Bobby this is the book of life, this book was given to us by God and it is called the Bible. If we want to find out how to live, this is the book to read for it is timeless, it never gets old or out of date."The Bible's knowledge to help you with others who lie and try to hurt you is right here in the Ten Commandments; they never get old and are timeless for all to follow.

That was the beginning so many years ago of many Saturdays with his grandma, helping her in her yard, swinging on her porch looking up passages in the Bible and talking about important things to Bobby

Darrol, she always listened and cared about what he thought, grandmas are so special. He would cherish these talks and later realize she made a big difference in his life by giving him the Bible and a Christian understanding.

Listening to That "Little Voice"

Have you ever done something you know you shouldn't be doing but just before you did you stopped for a moment and hesitated for some reason? Perhaps you said to yourself, "Don't do this" or "Why am I doing this?" or maybe you thought "I shouldn't be doing this."

Have you heard someone say, "I should have listened to that little voice in my head?" Do some people really have a little voice in their heads? Most people don't actually hear a voice saying anything but for many it is more like a feeling. It can be hard to talk about feelings so someone used the term "a little voice in my head."

Actually this is what we call conscience or knowing right from wrong. Somehow when we get into trouble with our parents or other adults for something we shouldn't have done we seem to know before we did it that it was wrong. Mom or dad was certain to "cloud up and rain" on us usually grounding us or worse!

Four neighborhood boys were playing "cars" in a field making small roads for their toy vehicles pretending they were driving. One said, "Let's go into town and steal some toy cars and trucks so we will have more to play with." The boys all wanted more cars on their little dirt roads. The boys rode their bikes into town and went into the small store that carried toys and began looking at all the many wonderful toy trucks and cars. They all had agreed to take one and hide it in their pockets and leave.

After all four of them had taken some toys, one boy said he didn't feel right taking the toys and took it right back putting it back on the shelf. One of the other boys, although he loved the little toy car he stole because his parents couldn't buy him many toys, said to the others that after he took it he didn't get much enjoyment out of it and felt really bad. Later that day he told his parents and they took him back to the store so he could return it and he had to face the consequences, he was grounded and had extra chores to do.

Two of these boys experienced conscience, and knew what they were doing wasn't right. What about the two boys who didn't take the toys back? Didn't they have consciences too? Most likely they did have some conscience but some learn to listen to "that small voice" and some have to learn it the hard way.

Some have parents and grandparents that teach and model right from wrong. Perhaps the boys who observed family members appropriate actions had their "little voice" speaking to them. What we see we often do however we all learn about consequences of our behaviors and what responsibility means.

God gave us the Bible to help us understand what is right and what is wrong. He also gave us our parents to help us learn all of this. Did you know that the Bible has Ten Commandments that are there for all of us to learn this and other important lessons of life? One of the commandments says that we shouldn't steal or take what does not belong to us. The Ten Commandments are there to develop that small voice to take heed of the Lord's direction for our life.

Of Land Mines and Cardboard Houses

One afternoon, a small boy (somewhere in the Balkans) noticed some small pieces of scrap metal behind the wall of his home.

Much of his home was made of nothing more than cardboard and scrap lumber added on to mud walls. He thought he would remove the debris behind the wall perhaps there was something the family could use and he wanted to please his mother. The moment he picked up one of the pieces, there was a blinding explosion and then absolute darkness. The boy was unconscious. He had picked up a small antipersonnel land mine. It exploded, costing the boy both hands and left eye. His grandmother, who saw all this happen, ran to him hugging him in his burning, bloodied clothes. To her he was dead but the Lord had other plans for this youngster and he survived like so many others worldwide who have been maimed by land mines. The problem of land minds is not just isolated in this boy's world but is a daily problem in some eighty countries where daily life in the city and rural areas is a struggle.

What kind of life does a child like this lead, what kind of city would allow unexploded ordinance to just lie around? Those in the western and developed world know little of this boy's world.

In the boy's town streets are littered with garbage and potholes. Herds of animals have to be negotiated as vehicles make their way through the clogged streets. There are few traffic signals and many simply do not work. Power and water outages are a daily routine. A large crater-like hole was just adjacent to the modern hotel; such was the way of life for youngsters in this and many other cities that have lived with decades of war. What had been the start of a new building ended up as an abandoned hole in the center of the city, the developer gone with all the funding for the project. The entire country was constantly on the brink of economic collapse. Corruption is rampant and crime a constant worry.

Along the river that runs through the edge of town are houses literally made primarily of cardboard with discarded plastic on the roofs to keep out the weather. Often no heat is available and the only access to any water comes from the river that is polluted and offers only sickness to those drinking from it. An atmosphere of hopelessness pervades the city, engulfs it like a shroud of fog despite the sun and pristine mountains surrounding the boy's homeland.

These scenes are replayed day in and day out in towns and cities of all sizes in Third World countries that have emerged from civil war, regional wars or ethnic conflicts. Often few in these countries can even remember why some of the conflicts started. Children of all ages struggle just to survive. What can you do, what can we do? We can give of our resources, gifts and pray first. For some of us, we can go and work directly within these nations as disciples.

Jesus Christ commands us in Matthew to go and make disciples and to bring peace and the good news to those who have not heard the words of hope:

> *Therefore go and make disciples of all nations, baptizing them in the name of the Father and of the Son and of the Holy Spirit and teaching them to obey everything I have commanded you. And surely I am with you always to the very end of the age.*
>
> *Matthew 28:19*

Grandma and the Bible

Little Victoria Ann sat totally enthralled next to her grandmother as her "grams" read from the big family Bible. Her big blue eyes were transfixed on every word, every expression grams made as she read. Her sandy colored hair fluttered softly in the cool breeze that came through the porch as she swung gently with her special grandmother on the green porch swing. The cool summer afternoon was quiet as grams soft voice, filled with love and caring spoke these ancient words of wisdom. After each passage, these two "girls," one very old and one very young shared their thoughts, their comments as they swung gently back and forth discussing the passage, the old helping the young to understand. Swinging slowly on the porch swing each was enjoying the other's company and sharing the Word of God.

Perhaps you have heard the Bible described as the book of life or the blueprint of how to live yet when we look at how big and it is so many pages and words that seem so strange to us, so we wonder, "How can I understand the Bible?" To try alone is a big task, for some almost an impossible task. The best way to start is to have someone read small parts to you; some of the famous stories in both the old and new testaments, then ask questions about the story. Get involved in a Sunday school class with others your age. Have your mother, father or grand parent read their favorite passages or stories to you. Pick a time each day or each week and spend time first hearing the story and letting your "mind's eye" picture what is happening. Always keep some possible questions in mind. What is the purpose of this passage? What can we learn from this verse or story? How can this help me today? Everyone loves a good story, an exciting story with action and suspense. The Bible is full of exciting true stories, stories from God. The Bible is the Word of God for man! Most of these stories have a lesson that we can apply to how we live today. We may have all kinds of electronic games, television, movies and equipment but the simple stories and passages of the Bible still apply today in how we treat others, how we work and go about our daily life. Remove all of our modern devices that make life easier and more entertaining and we discover we are just like those in the Bible, people needing to know how to live and enjoy life. Quietly swinging on that Nebraska porch one summer day long ago, little Victoria Ann was learning how to live her life, be of service to others and use the Bible as the source of all understanding.

Unintended Consequences

Sometimes what we do in daily life has far-reaching consequences on so many others, unintended consequences that are least expected. Some unintended consequences are of a positive nature but some decisions, spoken words or actions have impacts on those we love and cherish in hurtful negative ways. The following story about Susie is just one small example.

Susie was a stubborn independent girl, she had a mind of her own and she seemed more often than not to always end up doing what she wanted with her friends and sometimes her family. Basically her family saw that she had a loving heart. Her friends were often amazed that she could be so selfish one moment and so loving the next. Her mother always told her to be kind, calm and to share but at times all Susie could think about was getting her way doing what she wanted. She loved her family but didn't tell them in words as regularly as she should and often not in her actions.

She made her Bible class at church dislike her too, she didn't mean to but she wanted to be in charge, the center of all activities. When her friends and family would give her constructive criticism she felt they were being mean to her. She knew how Christ had lived, God coming to earth as a man and dying for the world but Susie didn't really fully understand how important Christ was to the world. It seemed there were two forces within her both battling for control.

One day at school a boy Susie knew offered her a pink capsule that he said would make her feel good. Sure Susie had heard about not taking drugs but this looked like a piece of candy and in her mind she thought one wouldn't hurt. She was bound and determined to have things her way. Had her mother, father and teachers' talk of drugs really been true? She didn't think the stories were true so she took the pill.

Later that day she woke up in the hospital and couldn't understand for a moment where she was! She wondered why she was there. She was at school one moment and the next she was in the hospital with doctors and nurses hovering over her and she felt terribly sick. Her mother and father were there and they were crying and praying. They were not mad but concerned for Susie they loved her so much. Susie could be so funny and delightful to be around and her teachers and family are so proud of her when she applies herself and cooperates! The Lord had given her a second chance!

What are the unintended consequences here? Susie knew she shouldn't take drugs but she thought this one time wouldn't matter but it did. Another unintended consequence was her severe reaction, her almost dying in the hospital. The fact such a pretty talented girl almost lost her life because she wouldn't listen to her parents was indeed a serious unintended consequence.

The Bible is the blueprint for life. Reading Ephesians 6:1-3:

"Children, obey your parents in the Lord, for this is right. 'Honor your father and mother'– which is the first commandment with a promise that it may go well with you and that you may enjoy long life on the earth."

Susie learned a lesson and gained much knowledge about living, loving her family and following the Lord.

He Kicked the Bus Tires

His father, dressed in his railroad bib overalls, walked around the bus as if looking for a problem and excuse to not let his son leave, he kicked the tires, looked closely at the rear engine compartment as the engine hummed. The bus was idling as passengers slowly boarded. The bus was in good mechanical condition.

The father looked up at his son's face looking back at him with apprehension. His mother, two brothers and sister stared in disbelieve, her oldest child and their oldest brother was really leaving home. No one seemed to want him to go but he had graduated from high school and needed to move on into adulthood, he couldn't stay, there were no jobs in his small economically depressed hometown. He wanted to go to college but his parents couldn't afford to send him and he didn't know what he wanted to study anyway. The military offered training and adventure, yet he was terrified, he had never ventured more than a few hundred miles from home before and he always had his family to discuss the trials and tribulations of growing up. He was the oldest so he had to show the others the way.

His mother fought back tears, his brothers and sister looked on in dismay. His father had always said, rather emphatically, "When you're eighteen out you go; you have to learn to stand on your own two feet!" Somehow, his father's words were hollow and unmeaning that day. As he watched his father checking out the bus, his actions certainly didn't match that emphatic declaration. As tough as his "dad" was, he knew in his heart his dad loved him. He could see a tear and sadness on his dad's weathered and worn railroad face but raising four children is no easy task. He did all that he could to set his son on the right course trying to play "tough" but inside his son seemed to know he was a soft and loving father that knew the world was not soft and loving.

As the bus pulled away from the station and slowly turned the corner he looked out and saw his family standing together hanging on each other by his dad's old jalopy, alone in the parking lot looking forlorn. At that moment he really felt his parents love for him. All the rules his parents had were for a reason.

The Bible in 1 Corinthians 13: 8 says,

"Love never fails." 1 Corinthians 13:11 sums up leaving home well, "When I was a child, I talked like a child, I thought like a child, I reasoned like a child. When I became a man, I put childish ways behind me."

Leaving home and facing the adventure of life is easier when we know our Lord Jesus Christ is by our side.

Those on the Margins of Society

The boy was shivering, looked poor and isolated himself from the others on the playground. Most played around him and ignored him, he had no coat, and the weather was bitterly cold. The school wouldn't open for another forty-five minutes. No one wanted to talk to him, to play with him, no one seemed to care. I was in the fifth grade at the time and the little boy in the third grade. I knew where the boy lived so when I got home that day I told my mother about him. We were not rich but I implored my mother to find a coat for this boy. We found one of my old coats that didn't fit me any more, my mother was saving it for my little brother but we took it to the boy's home and I gave it to his mother. She was so thankful, she seemed a little embarrassed but also shocked that anyone would care.

Everywhere, not only in this country but all over the world there are peoples for some historical reason, from poverty, from war or from reasons we can't comprehend are isolated from those around them. I always seem to notice, do you? Whether it be those in our schools, communities or worldwide there are always those that need the support of others in society.

> *Speak up for those who cannot speak for themselves, for the rights of all who are destitute.*
>
> *Proverbs 31:8*

The isolated, marginal peoples of the world have so many needs, medical, nutritional, physical, financial and just plain everyday necessities we take for granted in the United States. We all see the advertisements on television and read about those in need in far away places, so many needs…we can become hardened in our hearts and minds. Others will help; I can't do anything, but others will, may be our thoughts. There are always little things one can do. Donations during a time of national disaster, donations of clothing to a number of organizations, time as volunteers and yes money if we have some. We all can help when called upon by our conscience and we need not forget the many scriptures of God.

> *The Lord raises the poor from the dust and lifts the needy from the ash heap.*
>
> *1 Samuel 2:8*

The Holy Spirit gives us a desire to connect, to witness in small ways. We should not forget about prayer. Prayer makes a big difference. Many church congregations have prayer teams that pray for marginalized peoples. Jesus spent two thirds of his time healing the sick helping those on the margins of society. We can all help those in our own small ways that are marginalized, who live on the edge of society here in our local communities and abroad. Prayer is the first and most important step on the way to helping those on the edge of society.

> *When he saw the crowd, Jesus had compassion on them, because they were harassed and helpless, like sheep without a shepherd. Then he said to his disciples, "The harvest is plentiful but the workers are few. Ask the Lord of the harvest therefore, to send out workers into his harvest field."*
>
> *Matthew 9:36-37*

The next day the little boy had on my old coat and smiled at me!

We Are Witnesses for Christ in All that We Do

Religion is a way of life, a label many choose for themselves. Jesus is a person; **_the Person_** who pulls us out of eternal death. Peter, Andrew, James and John did not call themselves Christians. They went about healing and preaching about the son of man and as they did they were watched and listened to even in the smallest of activities of their lives. So indeed, as Christians, we are witnesses to Christ in all that we do everyday as we go about our lives meeting and talking with others.

Jesus Himself said,

> *"But you will receive power when the Holy Spirit comes on you; and you will be my witnesses in Jerusalem, and in all Judea and Samaria and to the ends of the earth"*

Acts 1:8

To be a witness for Christ, one has to live the life of Christ everyday in all that we do and say, a big job since we all have come short of the glory of God and live in a world full of evil. So we must arm ourselves in our minds and hearts to do as Jesus did because we don't know who may ask us questions or see us as we interact with others. In many instances, we may not even know we are being watched, that we are being witnesses for Christ. So we must avoid the temptations that come our way and be constantly aware of how we behave no matter where we are or what we are doing, working, having fun or just going about the daily chores of life!

There once was an American, a Christian working in the Balkans amid many unbelievers and others of different faiths. He was working in a secular job and was not a missionary. One day, one of the interpreters asked the Christian if she could ask him a personal question. He said yes not knowing what she might ask. She simply asked him why was he the way he was? At first he didn't understand but as they talked, she wanted to know why he seemed so at peace, calm, had a sense of humor in the difficult and dangerous situations in which they worked and was trusting. He accepted everyone that he met offering them his help in the tasks at hand. He said he would answer the question but that she should not be offended in what he said. She readily agreed. He told her he was a Christian. The interpreter was of the Muslim faith and had never been around any Christians before. This encounter started a conversation about Christianity that he didn't expect as he had not said anything about his faith, in fact he had been instructed not to preach or speak of his faith in this secular job. What was it that she saw in him? Was it the Holy Spirit? I believe it was, and she had been watching all that he did in the day to day activities of the jobs at hand.

How do you behave when you leave church? Are you aware of those around you that may be unbelievers? We are all called to use our gifts, for some they become pastors, missionaries, and Christian workers but for most of us we lead simple lives, everyday lives going to work, or school. For many Christians, they seek out others and witness to them directly about Christ but for most of us we may only get to talk about our faith occasionally so as you pray, ask the Lord to guide you in your actions and your words. Don't be afraid to be a witness but seek the Lord's guidance that you will be a worthy witness speaking what the Holy Spirit puts into your heart so that you will be a witness for Christ in all that you do.

What Does Being Humble Mean?

Looking up the word humble in various dictionaries one finds that it simply means to reduce pride or arrogance, to be marked by modesty, being unpretentious in character. Have you ever heard someone say "act big" or "talk big"? Trying to act important for attention is acting big or talking big. If you have seen someone who tries to act big then you have an idea of arrogance or being proud and self centered all of which goes counter to being humble. Perhaps you have met someone like this and you noticed they didn't act like they cared much for others. Maybe they are working so hard to seem important they don't notice the needs of those around them. We all need to develop self confidence and be able to tackle any new problems life offers but at the same time be humble and of service to others. Knowing what being humble means can help all of us better understand the difference between arrogance and humbleness. Self confidence also means not thinking of yourself more highly than you should but evaluating yourself and the gifts God has given you. Checking our blue print for life, the Bible, we can learn more about being humble.

Be completely humble and gentle; be patient, bearing with one another in love.

Ephesians 4:2

Humble yourselves, therefore, under God's mighty hand, that he may lift you up in due time.

1 Peter 5:6

Jesus said:

Therefore, whoever humbles himself like this child is the greatest in the kingdom of heaven.

Matthew 18:4

Take my yoke upon you and learn from, for I am gentle and humble in heart, and you will find rest for your souls.

Matthew 11:29

For everyone who exalts himself will be humbled, and he who humbles himself will be exalted.

Luke 14: 11

Even in the Old Testament we find references to being humble.

He [God] guides the humble in what is right and teaches them his way.

Psalm 25:9

For the Lord takes delight in his people; he crowns the humble with salvation.

Psalm 149:4

He [God] mocks proud mockers but gives grace to the humble.

Proverbs 3:34

Being humble can help open your mind to new learning, understandings, wisdom and yes love! And remember:

"God opposes the proud but gives grace to the humble"

James 4:6

How Important Is Attitude in Life?

We have all heard someone say he or she has "attitude." What is attitude and how important is it in life? Looking up this word, the dictionary definition that has the most meaning to life is: "A state of mind or feeling with regard to a matter." What is in the Bible regarding attitude and what state of mind is Christ like?

> *For the word of God is living and active. Sharper than any double-edged sword, it penetrates even to dividing soul and spirit, joints and marrow; it judges the thoughts and attitudes of the heart.*
>
> *Hebrews 4:12*

> *"In the beginning was the Word, and the Word was with God, and the Word was God"*
>
> *John 1: 1-2*

God's Word is God and it penetrates into our spirit and helps us judge our thoughts and attitudes. Strive to develop a positive attitude in all that you do and keep your mind focused on all that is good and pray to do God's will.

> *You were taught, with regard to your former way of life, to put off your old self, which is being corrupted by its deceitful desires; to be made new in the attitude of your minds; and to put on the new self, created to be like God in true righteousness and holiness.*
>
> *Ephesians 4: 22-23*

By accepting and believing in Jesus Christ we are commanded to put off our old ways and to have a new attitude in our minds and hearts, to be like God. How can we do this? After accepting Christ we need to pray always and seek His knowledge in His Word. We need to find a good church and to study and pray with others for guidance and to give thanks for all our blessings. We all have blessings no matter how dark and discouraged one gets. To have a godly attitude is to think of the blessings He has given us and to pray.

> *Your attitude should be the same as that of Christ Jesus... he humbled himself and became obedient to death even death on a cross!*
>
> *Philippians 2:5, 8*

> *Therefore, since Christ suffered in his body, arm yourselves also with the same attitude, because he who has suffered in his body is done with sin. As a result, he does not live the rest of his earthly life for evil human desires, but rather for the will of God.*
>
> *1 Peter 4:1-2*

Once we have humbled ourselves and become obedient we will not chase after worldly desires but through prayer seek God's way to be in His service. Developing an attitude of service to others and to the will of God is not an easy task but we need to be finished with sin in our attitudes, in our state of minds. Chasing after worldly desires doesn't mean we can't enjoy life and the pleasures of our jobs, our families, our hobbies. Notice the scripture in 1 Peter says we shouldn't seek out "evil human desires."

Becoming a Christian and accepting Christ will open the door to the Holy Spirit's seal and help.

Having believed, you were marked in him with a seal, the promised Holy Spirit, who is a deposit guaranteeing our inheritance until the redemption of those who are God's possession – to the praise of his glory.

Ephesians 1:13-14

But the fruit of the Spirit is love, joy, peace, patience, kindness, goodness, faithfulness, gentleness and self-control.

Galatians 5:22-23

We get our help and support from the Holy Spirit so we can focus on God and not seek deceitful desires of this life. We need to be diligent in forming our perspectives of this world for we are in the world but not of the world because we have sought after Christ. We can have our every desire but also at the same time be in His service and seek His ways and will. This is through prayer and study of the Word of God!

Put on your new self, your new attitude and feelings in regard to this new life in Christ Jesus. The Holy Spirit is in you as a help and guidance. Never forget what is in Hebrews, "…the Word of God is living and active," so seek it out daily to fuel your attitude for each day.

A Father's Gift of Christianity to His Family

We often know about the great deeds and events, the heroic efforts of our founding fathers, the wonderful documents, the trials and tribulations but sometimes we overlook small insights into our famous founding fathers. Almost everyone knows who Patrick Henry of US history is but not many may know of one of his quotes that gives us additional insight into this family man. This obscure Patrick Henry quote of interest is:

> *"I have now disposed of all my property to my family. There is one thing more I wish I could give them, and that is the Christian religion. If they had that, and I had not given them one shilling, they would have been rich, and if they had not that, and I had given them all the world, they would be poor."*
>
> *Patrick Henry*

I found this tattered quote taken from a newspaper in my father's Bible after he died and it made a profound impact on me as I then saw what he was trying to share with his family as we were growing up. Despite all of the distractions of life, my dad's message got through to me and I accepted Jesus Christ as my Savior many years ago before I was twelve years old. Growing up I strayed from the teachings of Christ but later came back and also tried to instill in my children this wonderful gift of grace given to all mankind.

This gift of love from a father to his family in my mind has taken on a new meaning in this age of slick gadgets and materialism. Patrick Henry knew that had he not given his family members even one shilling or dollar but knew Christ, they would indeed be rich in so many other ways. He clearly states for all readers to consider that getting "all the world," all the riches one could imagine would ultimately mean his family would really be poor. He clearly understood that having Christianity was an incredible investment in the future, not only the physical future of his family's lives as they lived them here on earth but their future in eternity.

From time to time over the years since my father's death in 1973, I get my dad's worn Bible out and in the inside cover where he pasted this yellowed quote taken from a newspaper, I sit quietly and read it and consider how important what Patrick Henry said has been to my life. I think about my father and how, in his own crude loving way, he set about trying to be an example for his family. He gave me the gift of Christianity, a gift available for all, that God gave us through His son.

The Queen and the Other One

Three sisters grew up together. This story is about the oldest and the middle sisters. Every child is different and these three sisters are no exception. The oldest had trouble pronouncing the middle sister's name and somehow it came out "Queenie" and the nickname stuck. Of course as they grew older the nickname of Queenie was not in vogue so when her dad shortened it to "The Queen" she accepted the nickname and that is exactly how she came to be perceived. Because of sibling rivalry with the youngest sister The Queen developed a very independent tough side to her personality. Although she was a tough and independent self-starter she was also a very loving softhearted child with a personality that overflowed with sweet love and kindness for others. The youngest sister was a fireball and that is a story for another time!

The Queen's oldest sister often characterized herself as "The Other One" because of low self-esteem due to intense rivalry with the oldest sibling of the four, the first born brother. Now don't get me wrong, all four loved each other but all of them took different roads as often happens in families. The three sisters when young looked the same and because of their blond hair and blue eyes they were characterized as "The Viking Women" of the family.

The oldest and youngest children seemed to chart different and very independent courses leaving the two middle daughter to fend for themselves and yet grow close in their relationship. The oldest sister worked for a short time in a school for the handicapped developing a sensitivity for others with special needs. She was almost shy as she assisted and helped teach. On the other hand, The Queen was almost thrown in jail for assisting at a roadside accident where a truck driver needed medical assistance. She felt the police were not doing enough to get the ambulance to the accident scene and was berating the police for letting the driver lay on the ground without any medical attention. They became so angry they threatened to throw her in jail if she didn't shut up, so is the caring and love of The Queen.

How brothers and sisters treat each other can determine at least in part how siblings grow up and view themselves. Because of intense rivalry and even jealousy families can be fractured if they don't seek out the teachings of Jesus Christ and realize that He came into this world with a great love for God the father's children, mankind. The Other One, while loving, is self-deprecating while the middle sister developed a tough attitude about some aspects of life and yet is too a very loving and giving person. As you read this you may be wondering how this writer came to this knowledge about these two sisters that are bound by love for family and others.

This author is the father. He has a special bond with his daughters that is truly a gift from God and a treasure in his life. The daughter's names are Krystal (The Other One), Kurenia (The Queen) and Kandace (The Fire Ball), the Viking Women he loves and treasures. He now has two Viking grand daughters, Krystal (Sissy), Kristina (Bobina).

> *"Children's children are a crown to the aged, and parents are the pride of their children"*
>
> Proverbs 17:6

Living to see one's grandchildren is a great blessing indeed to a father.

Intelligence vs. Wisdom

What is the difference between intelligence and wisdom? Is there really any difference? The dictionary says intelligence is the ability or capability to perceive and comprehend meaning. Wisdom is defined as learning, insight, judgment, discretion and prudence with intelligence. Wisdom is the use of intelligence and learning with insight and caution. To learn but not be able to use it is useless. To understand its use is to have wisdom. Learning and wisdom go hand in hand. The Bible has a great deal of timely information on wisdom.

> *The quiet words of the wise are more to be heeded than the shouts of a ruler of fools. Wisdom is better than weapons of war...*
>
> *Ecclesiastes 9:17-18*

> *For the Lord gives wisdom, and from his mouth (God's Word) come knowledge and understanding.*
>
> *Proverbs 2:6*

So if you have good grades does that mean you also have wisdom? Good grades are one of the many steps toward wisdom, finding out as much as you can about the world, its people, history, about science and math. Just being smart, having intelligence, doesn't mean you are wise too but notice wisdom is also learning a special kind of sensitivity.

But even the wise who do not accept Christ will have their wisdom lost.

> *"I will destroy the wisdom of the wise; the intelligence of the intelligent I will frustrate. Where is the wise man? Where is the scholar? Has not God made foolish the wisdom of the world? For since in the wisdom of God the world through its wisdom did not know him..."*
>
> *1 Corinthians 1:19-21*

Learning that special sensitivity has a special responsibility to not only our fellow man but to God as well, seeking out what God wants us to learn and do through prayer.

Even Jesus knew that wisdom and learning come from God and should be used to better understand God and his purposes. Jesus said,

> *"I praise you, Father, Lord of heaven and earth, because you have hidden these things from the wise and learned, and revealed them to little children"*
>
> *Luke 10: 21*

Jesus said to His disciples,

> *"Blessed are the eyes that see what you see. For I tell you that many prophets and kings wanted to see what you see but did not see it, and to hear what you hear but did not hear it"*
>
> *Luke 10: 23-24*

> *"...You have known the holy Scriptures, which are able to make you wise for salvation through faith in Christ Jesus"*
>
> *2 Timothy 3:14*

We must seek God through Jesus Christ, pray for guidance so we can learn to use our intelligence, to become wise in the ways of God.

> *"The fear of the Lord is the beginning of wisdom; all who follow his precepts have good understanding. To him belongs eternal praise"*
>
> Psalm 111:10

Being wise and using all you have learned involves more than some realize but through prayer, faith and understanding our Lord Jesus Christ will show the way, show you the ways of wisdom.

God Is a Healing God

The Bible says God is a healing God. When he speaks to us it is not so we can physically hear him. He speaks to us through His Word! Our Lord can heal us, His Word is our healing.

"For I am the Lord, who heals you"

Exodus 15:26

"He [God] heals the brokenhearted and binds up their wounds"

Psalm 147:3

His grace and healing comes to us through His Word. Just what is grace? Grace is an undeserved gift.

"This is what the Lord says:...For I know the plans I have for you, declares the Lord, plans to prosper you and not to harm you, plans to give you hope and a future. Then you will call upon me and come and pray to me, and I will listen to you"

Jeremiah 29: 10-12

> "For the law was given through Moses; grace and truth came through Jesus Christ"
>
> *John 1:17*

> "Therefore, since we have been justified through faith, we have peace with God through our Lord Jesus Christ, through whom we have gained access by faith into this grace in which we now stand"
>
> *Romans 5: 1-2*

Seek out the Lord in prayer and understand that Jesus said that in this world there will be trouble. Trust the Lord and remember,

> "Have I not commanded you? Be strong and of good courage; do not be afraid, nor be dismayed, for the Lord your God is with you wherever you go"
>
> *Joshua 1: 9*

> "And we know that all things work together for good to those who love God, to those who are the called according to His purpose"
>
> *Romans 8:28*

With promises like these how can we not trust in God as a healing God?

> "What then shall we say to these things? If God is for us, who can be against us? He who did not spare His own Son, but delivered Him up for us all, how shall He not with Him also freely give us all things"
>
> *Romans 8: 31-32*

> "Therefore take up the whole armor of God, that you may be able to withstand the evil day, and having done all, to stand"
>
> *Ephesians 6:13*

"...Above all, taking the shield of faith with which you will be able to quench all the fiery darts of the wicked one"

Ephesians 6:16

We must pray daily asking for God's guidance and healing based on His promises.

The Green Porch Swing

I remember my grandmother's screened-in porch. What a neat place to sit on a warm summer's night or a sunny Sunday afternoon. The main item on her porch was a wooden green porch swing suspended by chains from the ceiling. As we rocked to the strange squeaking noise of the chains, we would talk and soak up grandma's life experiences. I think my grandma sat there with all of her grand kids at some time in their young lives. She even rocked some of her great grand children on that swing in our small town in Nebraska. She lived at 375 N. Kimball Street just off of Fourth Street. You could see the John Deer tractor dealer on the corner from her porch. Old Fourth Street still had the old brick paving so you could hear the cars and farm trucks ever so often rumbling and bouncing down the street. Our town was a small place with the main business being agriculture and the railroad. But that old green porch swing is in my memory most of all because that is where all of us grand kids soaked up the experiences and knowledge of Grandma.

  She would bake fresh bread in the summer and we would sit on that porch and talk about life. We would drink ice tea and she would share her thoughts and love with us always gently pointing us in the right directions of growing up. I guess that is where I got my respect and admiration for my grandma. She was a wise soul that had story and an answer for every bump in the road the grand kids faced in their young lives. We would threaten to run away to grandma's house because she understood us and would listen. Many of her stories and experiences came from the ranch she grew up on in western Nebraska in the small sand hills town of Oconto. But most of all grandma told us stories from the Bible. She instilled in her grandkids a Christian desire to know Christ and serve others without us even knowing she was having such a major influence.

Grandmas are special and for some kids growing up they don't realize how much they can learn from grand parents. Our grandma was widely read and knew what was happening in the news here and around the world. We all thought she knew everything. She would insist that we all do well in school because she said a good education would get us far in this world so we all would from time to time bring her some of our school art work and papers to see. She was most interested in how we were doing. She used to say she didn't have the opportunities that we would have if we stayed in school. We knew in our hearts she was probably the smartest lady on the earth. And could she cook too! She worked in a boardinghouse cooking meals for ranch hands and railroaders. She used to say, "You could get a meal for $.15 cents in those days!"

After Grandpa died, I used to take off from my job almost every day for over a month to visit her at her house to help her grieve her loss. Some times I would have a quick lunch with her and we would sit on the green porch swing. She said she was very proud of me for graduating from college and becoming a teacher and being in the military reserve too. I could not have done it without her encouragement and love, she really taught me about life.

When we had all grown up and were off on our own life adventures we would always keep in contact with Grandma. After I had served a stint in the military and had returned to go to college I was shocked to discover Grandma had only an *eighth grade education*, she was so wise, how could that be? I then realized why she had insisted we all finish school. She knew that without an education we would be limited in our opportunities but I also then realized that while school was important, there was so much more to learn about life and being of service to others. She has been gone now for over twenty years but I still often sit and think of her in my quiet moments. After she died at age eighty-four, I realized I would not have gotten where I had in my life without her. Yes, my parents were important too, but grandmas and grandpas are special, they can make a difference in a family and they do every day. What have you learned from your grandpa or grandma? Have you hugged your grandma today?

Accepting Christ as Your Savior

What happens when you accept Christ and choose to follow Him? This can be confusing seeing pastors on television and even in church talking about accepting Christ as our Savior. Some do a great job of explaining and some don't. Some evangelists and their organization are superb in follow-up because a new believer is vulnerable to the old life and needs guidance and understanding. A new believer needs to be mentored in his or her beginning walk with Christ. The new believer's vulnerability is in the fact that Satan doesn't want us to be saved and puts up all kinds of attacks, distractions and roadblocks to a walk with our Savior.

Jesus Christ died for our sins. All we have to do is accept Him.

"For Christ died for sins <u>once for all</u>…to bring you to God"

1 Peter 3:18

"If we confess our sins, he is faithful and just and will forgive us our sins…"

1 John 1:9

I asked Him to come into my life, to lead my life and to forgive me of my sins. So, what is sin?

"All wrongdoing is sin..."

1 John 5:17

The dictionary says sin is breaking God's law. So what are His laws? Begin to understand His laws by reading the Ten Commandments in God's Word, the Bible. There may be only 10 but they can set the stage for our lifetime of behaviors. All of mankind falls short in keeping God's laws.

"For all have sinned and fall short of the glory of God..."

Romans 3:23

This story is my brief account of how I was saved and what I felt and how my young life's direction was so positively altered after my acceptance of Christ into my heart. I don't remember my exact age but I do remember I was about twelve or thirteen and lived in Nebraska. I remember our pastor at the time asked those wanting to have a walk with Christ to come down to the front of the church. My brother Don and I went down and the pastor prayed with us. I felt somehow, again I was very young, relieved that I would be a better son to my parents, I felt like a weight had been lifted from my shoulders, life had a new hope for me.

Shortly after my confession of sins and acceptance of Christ, my family went to a church camp in Colorado where I began to learn even more. I was enthused about the message and its power to change a person but upon our return home after the one week camp I felt our church didn't seem to care. Oh, I knew in my heart I was changed because of Jesus but as I entered my teenage years I had little guidance and strayed away. My mother and father often didn't agree on church attendance or what was sometimes taught there. Seeing how this came between them affected me and I stayed away, my dad seemed to be the only one to attend church regularly. I did read the Bible but without guidance and help I was a ship without a rudder or direction. Anyone new to the walk with Christ needs guidance and mentoring for a time depending on the individual. My grandmother also planted the seeds of Christianity and kept reminding me in her gentle loving way her whole life as only grandmothers can seem to do.

Our modern society has a way of trivializing Christianity, degrading a belief in Christ to the point of being ashamed of not "fitting in" to modern thinking or even being ashamed of believing in Jesus. Our materialistic existence is constantly making us selfish. We need to understand how to serve others. Everywhere I turned I was confronted with the idea believing in Christ was out of step. The attack on my belief and faith was at every turn I chose in life. I became too competitive always seeking to be first, always achieving, succeeding. I finally realized that I must serve others I went to college and became a teacher. It took me a long time to realize my gift was teaching and serving others not to compete, to win, to get, to have. Jesus said.

> *"But many who are first will be last, and many who are last will be first"*
>
> *Matthew 19:30*

When I joined the US Air Force after high school, I was given a small blue Air Force Bible that brought me back to at least a study of the Bible again. I carried that small blue Bible with me for many years. It wasn't until I had my own children that I knew how important regular worship and Bible study is for everyone, every Christian. Ironically, it was my son who got me back to church as he became quite active in our local church's youth group.

In years past, I made the mistake of always looking at others that attended church, judging them for what I knew about some of them and that is wrong. We should attend church and seek fellowship and guidance for ourselves to serve others to do His will, to pray always and ask for guidance in our lives to do His work as He directs us. We should <u>never be envious or judge others.</u> Jesus said,

> *"Do not judge, or you too will be judged"*
>
> *Matthew 7:1*

This is a powerful instruction.

Though I never strayed far I still strayed, the Lord wasn't able to use me to His fullest, I was susceptible to the glitter and glamour of our world, the workaholic succeed, get, accomplish. He will give you all these things if you seek Him first. Jesus said,

> *"Ask and it will be given to you, seek and you will find; knock and the door will be opened to you. For everyone who asks receives; he who seeks finds; and to him who knocks, the door will be opened"*
>
> *Matthew 7:7-8*

Even though I strayed He guided my life and my experiences. He has a plan for all of us; we just have to repent, study His Word, pray and be patient as we wait on the Lord. Everything we need is in His Word! My time serving in the military and as a teacher, though not seeking Him and praying daily, my life was still directed by Him. As I look back, I realize the opportunities given me were all from the Lord, my successes were not of my making but of His because I committed myself to Him so many years ago. He knew I would return to a closer walk with Him. Don't do as I did, commit yourself now and follow Him all your life, pray for help to fight the distractions of our world, the sin, the temptations and serve Him and others diligently.

Christ said,

> *"Come to me, all you who are weary and burdened, and I will give you rest" "Take my yoke upon you and learn from me, for I am gentle and humble in heart, and you will find rest for your souls"*
>
> *Matthew 11:28, 29*

But we all have to take that first step, to ask for forgiveness and to seek our Lord Jesus Christ but also to be ready for the distractions, to be ready to focus and seek His guidance in His Word the Bible. We must pray unceasingly.

> *"...Pray continually; give thanks in all circumstances, for this is God's will for you in Christ Jesus"*
>
> 1 Thessalonians 5:16

If you are a new Christian, or haven't yet repented, seek out guidance, find a church and simply put your trust in our Lord Jesus Christ, His teachings are timeless. Do you want a positive future, a future of hope? All you have to do is pray for forgiveness and commit yourself to Jesus Christ.

A Father and Son Revelation

I was an Air Force major in 1990 in the midst of the demanding ten month Air Command and Staff College (ACSC) course of study when I received a call from my son Scott. He wanted to drive from Nebraska to Maxwell AFB in Montgomery, Alabama, to see me. He would only get to visit for a week. I made it clear that I couldn't take any time off but would love to see him. I asked Scott if he was bringing a girlfriend or coming alone because the apartment I shared with another major was only two bedrooms and quite small. He was driving by himself. We both were excited at seeing each other.

When Scott arrived I had arranged for him to sleep on the couch and got him permission to visit the college and sit in on some of the joint open and unclassified sessions where all 600 national and international military students attended. Scott was able to make the rounds of Montgomery visiting some of the museums and the historic downtown area where Martin Luther King had his church and the famous bus boycott of the '60s took place. He visited the Shakespeare Festival and we were able to attend an evening play together. For the most part Scott explored the surrounding areas of Montgomery and Selma, Alabama soaking up all the southern history.

Scott was there for only a week and each evening his three sisters and mother called to talk to me and Scott. "Have you talked to him yet?" "When are you guys going to sit down and talk? He has something to tell you." I said we would talk and spend time together but as the week wore on there always seemed to be more activities and distractions than planned. Even when there was a break there was an air of uncomfort, an awkwardness of impending information that no one wanted to talk about. Still, we each enjoyed each other's company because we are alike in many respects and have many of the same interests, science fiction, advertising, writing, and teaching. We are close as a father and son.

On the night before Scott's last day my ex-wife Karen, Scott's mother, called again and finally blurted out, "You know Scott is gay?" Taken a little by surprise I replied, "I had suspected something like that. So this is what we have to talk about?" He had no sooner hung up when his oldest daughter called and asked if I had talked to Scott yet. The whole family was on pins and needles because so often when a father, a conservative military father, finds out this kind of information there can be serious repercussions and reactions. Literature is full of parents disowning their children, kicking them out of the home or worse when they find out a son or daughter is homosexual; this is especially true for fathers it seems.

The last night of Scott's visit came. My roommate was gone for the evening so Scott and I were alone. Scott's bags were packed, the TV was off. We sat and visited quietly. Suddenly there was a silence, a long silence. Finally after what seemed like many minutes, I said, "I understand we are supposed to talk." Scott said, "Yes, we do need to talk." I looked pensively at the floor and began, "I understand you have a propensity for homosexuality?" There was a stunned silence as Scott looked up into his dad's face and said, "Yes, Dad, I am gay!" My eyes filled with tears as I said, "I don't understand it all, Scott, but I want you to know I still love you and am here for you as always." Both began to cry, they stood up and hugged each other both sobbing quietly.

The rest of the evening was spent talking about what all this meant. We both had to laugh because not only had all three of Scott's sisters and mother called me but they had been frequently calling Scott on his cell phone too! We both were uncomfortable and didn't know how the other would react. We were so relieved when it was out in the open and we could finally talk about it. Scott was relieved because I didn't react negatively but affirmed my love for him. This indeed was a father and son revelation, a point of determination of what the future possibly would hold for both of us since we were talking, processing and most importantly we still loved each other. The future didn't look all that uncertain now but we certainly had a lot to discuss and sort out.

I love the Lord and in my heart I know

> *"...that in all things God works for the good of those who love him..." (Romans 8:28). "Fathers do not embitter your children or they will become discouraged"*
>
> *Colossians 3:21*

In this father and son revelation, we both began to forge ahead, to discuss to keep on loving each other for

> *"...parents are the pride of their children"*
>
> *Proverbs 17:6*

A Ham Sandwich and Coffee!

My dad served in WWII in the Army Air Corps as a fireman. He recounted a story about being on guard duty one night somewhere at an Army post in the US. He was at his post when an official Military Police Truck came in with a load of GI prisoners, fellow troops that had gotten into some type of trouble and had to serve some brig time. His job was to escort them to the Brig but they had been on the road all day and without any rations or food stops. They were all cold and very hungry. The drivers were indifferent, they were prisoners. My dad told them the chow hall had closed, they were unhappy to say the least.

My dad got them into their cells and told them he would see what he could do for them. He had a friend who worked in the mess hall and went to him. Reluctantly he told my dad that he could make them some ham sandwiches and take them some coffee. There was always coffee brewing in the mess hall 24/7. My dad's friend unlocked the mess hall kitchen and found some sliced ham and bread. So my dad went to work making up a dozen ham sandwiches and found a portable coffee pot. He found other "leftover" items from the evening meal and loaded it up in a jeep and took it to the brig. There were some very happy, thankful and hungry GIs who quickly devoured the sandwiches and made quick work of the coffee and other goodies. My dad went back to his guard duty and never saw the men again.

About a year later my dad was on a ship transport going to the war in the Pacific. Late one night he was standing alone along the side of the ship watching the waves and night sky when another soldier came up to him and said hello. He asked my dad if he remembered him and my dad said no. The other soldier proceeded to tell him how he remembered him and how thankful he was for the ham sandwiches and coffee my dad had rustled up that cold winter evening long ago. He told my dad that he had made a tremendous difference to all of the prisoners that night and wanted to personally thank him for his thoughtfulness. He shook my dad's hand and left him standing alone looking at the dark sea churning past the ship.

After he left it suddenly occurred to my dad that had he just followed orders and locked up the prisoners that cold winter evening that soldier could have come up behind him and shoved him over board and no one would have known my dad was gone until it was too late to save him from the cold northern Pacific waters.

My father told me this story one evening to remind me that to be a good Christian a person has to be aware of others needs and to be of service to others in less fortunate circumstances of life. Would that individual pushed my dad overboard? He had been in the brig and could well have felt the need to "get even" for not being treated fairly. An act of kindness can mean so much to a person who is feeling abandoned and alone. The one doing the kindness may never know the extent of what it meant at the time. My dad was lucky to have found out that what he did made a difference.

We are commanded in the Bible to love our neighbor as yourself. Jesus tells the story of the Good Samaritan in Luke, a heart warming story of helping others in need. Two passersby failed to help a beaten and robbed man. The third man, a Samaritan, took pity on him. He bandaged his wounds and took him to an inn and paid the inn keeper so he could recuperate. Jesus asked,

> "Which of these three do you think was a neighbor to the man who fell into the hands of robbers?" The reply was the one who had mercy on him and Jesus told him, "Go and do likewise"

Luke 10:30-37

"Quiet, Be Still"

Jesus said,

"Quiet, be still"

Mark 4: 39

The wind and the waves obeyed Him and were quiet and still.

"He said to his disciples, 'Why are you so afraid? Do you still have no faith?'"

Mark 4:40

Our lives are often like the storm Jesus calmed, we have the winds and waves of life hurling us about amid all the distractions these modern times offer. We must all pause and call upon the Lord to help us to be quiet and still and ponder His love for us and the fact He wants only the best for us.

Yes we all get afraid and forget to take all our cares, all our disappointments, failings and requests to Him in prayer. How soon Jesus' disciples forgot this and how soon we too forget and think we can solve all our problems. Some think we shouldn't take all our requests to God in prayer but the Bible says we are to do just that!

> *"Do not be anxious about anything, but in everything, by prayer and petition, with thanksgiving, present your requests to God"*
>
> *Philippians 4:6*

Are you facing a problem in school, at home, or with friends? Does it feel like there is no way out, no answer to the problem? This is the exact time we need to pray to Him. A youth minister once said that God answers all prayer, either yes, no or grow! Perhaps when you have prayed before you felt no answers came but perhaps that was one of those "grow" times. We have to be patient and wait on the Lord, His time is not like our time.

> *I waited patiently for the Lord; he turned to me and heard my cry.*
>
> *Psalm 40:1*

> *Be joyful in hope, patient in affliction, faithful in prayer.*
>
> *Romans 12:12*

When we are young the word patience means waiting. The spirit of youth has trouble waiting because we live in a world of instant gratification, instant food, instant TV entertainment at our finger tips so we expect everything to come quickly but that is not how patience works. So what are we to do?

First, always pray no matter where you are, say a prayer to yourself in your thoughts as you walk between classes or on the way to school or while you wait for the bus. If you have a problem, talk with your parents or a teacher you trust of if your school has a counselor go see him or her. Often, someone else will have a different perspective that can help. None of us no matter our age can solve all our problems by ourselves, we all need help from time to time but we should never forget prayer.

Second, study God's Word. Read it by yourself or in a Bible study group at church. Discuss what His Word means to you in a group or think about it as you meditate by yourself.

Third, author Bruce Wilkinson in his little book entitled *Secrets of the Vine* recommends we get up early and read His Word and keep a journal as if we are talking to God. This is not a diary, but a journal of your thoughts to God as you seek Him and abide in Him and His Word.

"...He who abides in Me, and I in him, bears much fruit"

John 15:5

So don't be afraid, seek the quietness within your mind and be still, pray and trust in our Lord no matter the adversity, stress or suffering you are enduring.

Don't Be Ashamed

Why is it that we can wear polo shirts with logos announcing to the world the organizations we belong to or T-shirts with pictures of the places we have traveled to or even the disasters we have survived, yet we often shy away from those shirts that depict Jesus as our Savior? Some wear T-shirts telling the world they are Christians and believe in all the promises of Christ yet some seem ashamed to wear these. Yes many Christian youth groups have these shirts and many youth wear them but there are those who are Sunday Christians and for the rest of the week blend into the populace. Of course many don't want any attention and simply want to lead a private life. We all have to find out how we can best serve the Lord; the best way is through prayer. What are your talents? Pray that you will be given direction to use your talents and to do His will in your life.

What kind of Christian are you or are you even a Christian? Have you given your heart to Christ? If not, find a quiet room kneel and pray a simple prayer. "Lord Jesus, forgive me of my sins, come into my heart and direct my life. Help me to live the life you want direct all my ways." Any similar simple prayer is all that is needed, find a church and seek out guidance as a new Christian but most of all develop a perspective of sharing, realizing all the people you meet will see a difference in you.

Most of all realize some people will not understand your new found peace and some may even persecute you and make fun of you but don't lose sight of all the promises in scripture. Don't let persecution make you ashamed of being a Christian; it can happen over time and does for some new Christians. Because of persecution guard against becoming just a "Sunday Christian" and pray that you will be guided by His Word to use your talents to their fullest everyday for the glory of Jesus Christ our Savior.

Not everyone worships with the same kind of enthusiasm or in the same manner. We need to find out, through prayer, how we can best be a witness to Jesus Christ. In Romans 10:11 it says, *"For the Scripture says, 'Whoever believes on Him will not be put to shame.'"* So we must all be witnesses to those who have not believed and by our actions and by our words we say that there are glad tidings of good things in believing in our Lord Jesus Christ. Our salvation through the grace of Jesus Christ's sacrifice for us is God's salvation plan and that no one is ever to be excluded, it is available for all people of all nations and races.

Who then is bold enough to confess aloud that our Jesus is Lord? How else will those who have not heard the good news of Jesus Christ ever get the message or come to believe if we don't speak up and witness using our God given talents. So don't be ashamed, pray and discover through prayer what your role is to be in getting the message out to the world about Jesus Christ. Jesus said,

> *"If anyone is ashamed of me and my words, the Son of Man will be ashamed of him when He comes in his glory and in the glory of the Father and of the holy angels"*
>
> Luke 9:26

Forty Crosses

The busy traffic zoomed around the eleven Christians as they silently marched down the side of the Pan American Highway in Douglas, Arizona, moving slowly and deliberately toward the border. Curious on lookers walking and in cars slowed and stared as each Christian stopped and held up a small white cross and said the name of the deceased Mexican national that the cross represented, some represented undocumented remains, some were children. The cross was then placed against the curb in silent testimony for these needless deaths. The sight of these forty crosses stretched out for over two blocks in the setting Arizona sun evoked a lot of emotion. Only forty crosses to represent the hundreds of deaths that are occurring in our Arizona desert! Thousands have died just seeking jobs in the U.S.!

I took part in this prayer vigil one hot July afternoon and it was a trip I would not soon forget. For two blocks and for over an hour this weekly prayer vigil, conducted by Pastor Mark Adams of the Presbyterian Frontera de Cristo's "Healing our Borders" (HOB) ministry, marched slowly and prayed for the families of each of these lost individuals. Not only did the group pray for the families but for our governmental leaders on both sides of the border for improved bi-national relationships and for positive changes that will help end death in the desert. This seems to be an insurmountable problem that prayers to our Lord Jesus Christ can help resolve, hence the purpose for this weekly prayer vigil. Pastor Adams conducts this prayer vigil every week regardless of weather.

The small white crosses laying against the curb of the Pan American Highway in Douglas, Arizona are mute reminders of the hundreds of needless deaths that take place in our desert as our neighbors set out on the dangerous trek from Mexico to the U.S. hoping for a better life and income for their families. Every year the deaths climb due to the sustained record setting heat and the numbers of undocumented Mexican nationals seeking work here in the U.S.

During this weekly prayer vigil, we heard the news that a mother died three miles east of Douglas with her two children at her side, a twelve year-old and his four year-old brother. Some of Pastor Adams friends and supporters of this missionary work found the boys hugging each other and crying at a US Customs check point as they waited to be sent back to authorities in Mexico.

Healing Our Borders (HOB) is a Douglas, Arizona, and Agua Prieta, Sonora (in Mexico) based, interfaith group praying for all migrants, especially the families of those who have needlessly died in the desert and for families that have not heard from loved ones and do not know their whereabouts or conditions. HOB delivers blankets and other items needed by migrants. This ministry also cleans the deserts and lands of items that are left behind by these migrants in their desperate journey for a better life. And HOB tries to educate people on both sides of the border about the dangers of trying to trek across the desert. For many, coming from deep within the interior of Mexico such as the tropical Chiapas State where they only know the jungle and can't understand a desert with no rivers or lakes.

Pastor Adams' weekly prayer vigil is making a difference in Douglas. We all can get directly involved in missions for Christ, just look around you check out what your church is doing or just simply keep these people in your prayers. We are to make disciples for Christ and get the good news of salvation out to the world.

Our World's Forgotten People - The Unreached for Jesus Christ!

I hadn't been in Albania but a few hours when three small tattered and unkempt gypsy boys rushed up to our vehicle and kissed its fender and then proceeded to hold out their hands for money! I asked why they weren't in school and was told they are not allowed to go to school because they were gypsies. A quote from a Slovakian leader, Jozsef Pacal, mayor of Medzev, Slovakia, sums up the plight of all gypsies located worldwide: "I'm no racist, but some gypsies you just have to shoot." Gypsies are a classic example of marginalized, forgotten peoples in need of our prayers!

There are many other marginalized peoples in our world that go unnoticed besides the gypsies. Think for a moment about some one or some segment within our own country that exists on the margins of society. Dr. Samuel Hugh Moffatt, missionary to Korea, said, "Supportive prayer at the home base can be as important in Christian missions as direct Christian presence on the far-off frontiers."

So what should we do for the unreached? Find out what countries you want to pray for or get involved in your church's missions program. Become a part of the worldwide prayer movement for world evangelization. As you learn about unique peoples and cultures, pray for them and for our missionaries ministering to them.

"Three times a day he got down on his knees and prayed... just as he had done before"

Daniel 6:10

We find so many unchurched, unreached peoples needing prayer throughout the world. Mexico and the United States seem like "distant neighbors" yet no other countries that share such long borders differ so greatly in cultures. We think of Mexico as Spanish- speaking, but 7.5 million Mexicans speak as their mother tongue not Spanish but one of 290 indigenous languages. Many of these languages do not yet have a translated Bible or indigenous church. The non-Spanish speaking minorities tend to be trapped in poverty like so many of the unreached worldwide.

The small crying gypsy baby was in a cardboard box at the edge of a busy Tirana, Albania, street corner in freezing weather, its parents homeless. Passersby dropped coins in the box; this was how this gypsy family was attempting to survive. Gypsies gladly receive the good news of Jesus when it is presented to them with respect for the gypsy way of life. No longer homeless, in Jesus they can be citizens of earth and heaven. No longer despised, they can be honored and loved by God and their fellow man when they accept Jesus Christ into their lives.

Jesus said,

"Foxes have holes and birds of the air have nests, but the Son of Man has no place to lay his head"

Matthew 8:20

Become involved in the world wide prayer support for the unreached, check out how you can get involved in your church.

An Ancient Roman Disciple of Christ

The Roman centurion bent down over the bloody and bruised Roman Christian and looked into his eyes to see if there was a flicker of life. He thought to himself, "How could anyone live through this kind of torture and still be alive!" "What is it that makes these Christians so peaceful and what is that look in their eyes, like they see and know something that the rest of us are missing?" The Christian was still alive so he had him thrown back into his cell. Perhaps he would die peacefully in his painful sleep and save the Centurion the trouble of eventually having to execute him.

He knew he dare not try to investigate this Christian faith too closely or he would be in trouble with his commander. Still, the entire aura about these Christians in Rome haunted his thoughts by day and his dreams at night. He grew weary of having to capture them as they came out of the Roman catacombs and then eventually having to torture and execute them. He was a soldier, a warrior, a protector of all of what Rome had become to the world, a center of art and intelligence. He was not an executioner of innocent Roman citizens who chose to believe in a different God than what Rome decreed its citizens should believe. He wanted none of this but knew he had a good chance of being appointed to the Praetorian Guard that protected the emperor, a plum assignment meaning rapid promotion within the Roman Army. But he had to do all military jobs well to be considered for this assignment, even this most despicable job of overseeing the executions of Christians.

Petilius Caecilian was just vaguely aware of the centurion looking into his eyes. This centurion's eyes and demeanor seemed a little softer of mind than some of the other Roman soldiers. The pain was intense as they tossed him like a discarded rag into his cell. "Oh, sweet Jesus, forgive them as you forgave them from your cross!" He tried to concentrate on what he thought Jesus the Christ looked like to cloud the pain. In his mind's eye he seemed to see an outline of a face but could not discern the details, a bright light shone around his vision. Somehow this gave him a peace of mind, the pain was still there but held at a distance in the recesses of his brain.

How he wished his fellow Christians that were worshiping with him had gotten away, he knew not of their conditions or whereabouts as they all scattered about as they left the catacombs after a worship service. The Roman soldiers had been waiting for them as they emerged into the bright morning Italian sun. He thought perhaps he must have been the only one they caught since he stumbled and fell. He knew he had blocked the narrow alley for a moment giving the others time to blend into the early morning Roman crowds entering the market place. When was that? Was that yesterday or was that many days ago? The incessant torture and questioning by his captors was becoming a blur in his pain soaked mind.

As he lay in his cell he had time to contemplate the teachings of Christ he had learned to love and work at understanding so as to have a more righteous life. He had taken to heart the command by Matthew to make disciples of Christ that was why he was suffering now, the Roman government didn't want its citizens to have the peace of Christ. They didn't comprehend the grace and peace one can obtain from Christ. A sad note in its history but Petilius knew that before he died he was to make disciples of Christ. His every waking moment had been to live as Christ had lived. He often asked himself when facing adversity or decisions involving possible sin, "What would Jesus do?"

Petilius had a bright career ahead of him, possibly even a seat in the Roman Senate because of his family and its connections. His family was dismayed at his study and desire to learn more of this new religion called Christianity. Had he thrown all of this away in a vain study of a prophet who died on a Roman cross? He didn't think so because he felt a change come over him as he prayed and asked forgiveness accepting Jesus as his Savior. He willingly accepted Christ openly and publicly as his Savior and wanted to learn all that he could. His life took on a new meaning and vitality. He began attending the forbidden meetings in the Roman catacombs where he met other Christians like himself. He soon became known as a leader in this fledging religion that met and worshiped in the stench of the catacombs beneath Rome.

Petilius knew full well what was happening to the leaders of Christianity in Rome. Roman government targeted these individuals hoping to eventually destroy the church by eliminating it of its leaders. Some Christians sought out the torture and death in the arena to become martyrs but that was not the case for Petilius, he had a burning desire to follow the command to make disciples of Christ. His was a vision for the future, far more so than his fellow Christian's visions for Christianity in Rome.

He laid in intense pain throughout the night contemplating his death no doubt to occur soon. Would he be beheaded or burned alive, perhaps he would be sent to the arena? He knew his ribs must be broken as he tried to roll on to his side screaming uncontrollably. Many of his bones must be broken and his right foot was pointed in the wrong direction and numb. To alleviate this horror at his physical condition he began to pray in earnest to Jesus for deliverance and peace.

Morning rays of sunlight began to stream into his cell making the straw in his cell a strange yellow red color. Soon his tormenters would be back to question and torture him anew. He would have a trial and soon no doubt and then meet his sweet Jesus. The iron clanking sound signaled the return of his guards. It was the gentler centurion who had checked his condition after the last beating. He helped him painfully to his one good leg telling him today was his trial. Two other soldiers helped Petilius limp painfully on a makeshift crutch fashioned from a tree limb and given to him by the centurion.

Petilius was offered the opportunity to make a sacrifice to the Roman gods for the health of the emperor and to recant his association with Christianity and then be freed. His family had interceded for him no doubt. But he refused and was promptly and unceremoniously condemned to die in the arena. What the animals didn't finish off the Roman soldiers would with their swords. His arena was scheduled for this very day, this very afternoon.

Many Christians died with dignity while others suffered horrendously slow, brutal deaths. Petilius and another Christian were placed in the arena and a huge, maddened wild bull turned in on them. Petilius hobbled about painfully on the makeshift wooden crutch but could not get out of the way of the charging bull. The bull gored the one Christian promptly to death and then dragged Petilius attempting to gore him. The animal was clumsy and simply aggravated the already serious wounds of days of torture and beatings. He cried out in agony before regaining a semblance of control, lying in a crumpled heap with the tired, panting bull looking forlornly at him.

Roman soldiers were sent into finish him off. The point of a soldier's blade entered his throat and killed him cleanly. Finally, his agony over, he met his Savior and won his martyr's crown. Petilius Caecilian and other faceless and nameless disciples of the risen Christ were changing the face of Rome and the world.

Archeologists in the nineteenth century excavating the catacomb of the Roman Caecilian family uncovered a fragmentary piece of an ancient inscription near the grave of St. Cecilia. It simply said, "Petilius, he gave up his soul to God at the age of thirty-three years and six months." What tribulations do modern Christians suffer making disciples of Christ?

Do modern Christians of the twenty-first century even understand Jesus' command of Matthew 28:19-20,

> *"Go therefore and make disciples of all the nations, baptizing them in the name of the Father and of the Son and of the Holy Spirit, teaching them to observe all things that I have commanded you; and lo, I am with you always, even to the end of the age."*

What are you doing to make disciples for Christ?

CPSIA information can be obtained
at www.ICGtesting.com
Printed in the USA
FFHW020604080619
52892453-58473FF